Glory
WALKERS
REVEALED

SONYA L. THOMPSON

FOREWORD BY SHIRMEKA N. PEDEN

OIL & THE GLORY
PUBLISHING COMPANY
RELEASING HIS VOICE TO THE NATIONS

www.oilandtheglory.com

Oil &The Glory Publishing
Glory Walkers Revealed by: Sonya L. Thompson

This book or parts thereof may not be reproduced in any form, stored in retrieval system or transmitted in any form by any means - electronic, mechanical, photocopy, recording or otherwise - without prior written permission of the publisher, except as provide by United States of America copyright law.

Unless otherwise noted, all Scripture quotations are taken from the New King James Bible

ISBN-13: 978-0692526897
copyright ©2015 by Oil & The Glory Publishing

Cover Design by Oil & The Glory Publishing
www.oilandthglory.com

Table of Contents

DEDICATION

I dedicate this book to the following:

My Lord Jesus Christ, without whom I can do nothing. May you continue to use me for your glory.

To every Glory Walker who will be revealed as a result of reading this God breathed account. I celebrate your emergence from the tombs of religion and tradition as you embark on your journey with the Living God.

To my mom, Dorothy Walton. Thank you for standing by, encouraging and believing in me. Your love and support means everything to me. I love you.

To the memory of my grandmother, Cora Neal. The impact she had on my life is priceless. How I miss her and wish she could be here to share this moment with me. But, I rest assured that the Lord has shown her my favorable outcome. I can still hear her voice telling me, "You can do it!" Thank you Lord for the legacy this mighty woman of God has left me.

FOREWORD

By Shirmeka N. Peden

Hungry, craving, searching, seeking, panting and waiting are just a few of the words that can be used to describe those who are yearning to discover the glory and experience the authentic presence of God.

In this yearning, there is a sound being made in the earth and from the earth that connects to the heart and spirit of God. It is a sound of longing and desperation from His creation. A cry of desire to see the true and Living God breathe, move and abide within and among us, again. For some, it's a sound of holy frustration; the result of spiritual unrest. This unrest is birthed from the desire to simply see and experience more; more of His presence, more of His power, and more of His glory!

The question that permeates the heart of those experiencing such unrest is simple, yet compound; is this all there is? They have experienced meetings but not miracles, sermons but no signs and worship without wonders. They have experienced all that church has to offer. But, they have yet to experience the Living God.

Having written this book from the perspective of her own questioning, Sonya L. Thompson uses Glory Walkers Revealed not only to reveal the answer to this question from the Word of God; but to allow us an incredible opportunity to partake in her journey of experiencing more.

If you've been growing tired of the mechanics of church and have a desire not only to read the Bible but to see it come alive every single day of your life, then the words of this book will propel you into the tangible reality of the supernatural! As you read and explore the glory of God through the pages of this book, expect a great outpouring of His presence and power; which will thrust you into a brand new dimension and place. It is the dimension of the supernatural; an uncommon place of miracles, signs and wonders; the place of the Glory Walker Revealed!

INTRODUCTION

*"For the earth will be filled with the knowledge of
the glory of the Lord, As the waters cover the sea
(Habakkuk 2:14)."*

This book is an intimate and detailed account of what
happens when the cry of the spirit supersedes the
voice of religion and tradition. Glory Walkers Revealed
was birthed out of a heart which was desperately
longing for an intentional, repeated and uninterrupted
encounter with the Living God. During a time of reading
and study, I realized I held in my hands a Bible which
revealed a God of the supernatural. When compared
to my then, Christian existence, it fell far short of
the exploits of even my Old Testament forefathers;
not to even mention those of the New Testament. A
feeling of dis-ease settled in my spirit, until one day
like a man rising from sleep, I pulled back my spiritual
covers and arose from my slumber. I knew there had
to be more! I realized, to my amazement, a substitute
had taken place unawares. The presence and power
of God had been replaced with programs, religion
and tradition and was being presented as a genuine
encounter with the Living God! I had grown tired of

the mechanics of church, the absence of the presence of God and a demonstration of the power of the Holy Spirit. This discontentment grew so strong until it led me on a journey of panting and longing after God. As a result, one night, the Holy Spirit dropped two words into my spirit, **Azusa Street**. These two words sent me on a year-long pursuit of the God of the Bible. As a result, a divine appointment was arranged to meet with **Brother Tommy Welchel,** the last survivor who had received an impartation from many of the men and women involved in the **Azusa Street Revival**. In the end, I found myself taken from a place of dis-ease and discontentment to an unparalleled encounter with the Living God. I entered the realm of the glory, characterized by the manifest presence of God, with signs and wonders following.

I am confident that there is a cry of desperation arising from the hearts of believers across the nation. There is a cry in the wilderness that is going forth from the body of Christ from those who are also desperate and hungry for an intentional, repeated encounter with the Living God. It is a longing for the glory of God to be revealed in and through you. My friend you are not alone. God has reserved you for this hour. The Lord Jesus is as desperate as you are, to see you break free from the grasp of religion and tradition. He is looking for and longing for a people who will unashamedly arise and show forth His nature and character in the earth. I release a clarion call to you and the remnant, to *arise and shine for your light has come and the glory of the Lord has risen upon you!*

May this God breathed account cause your heart to burn within. May a fire ignite in you, sending you on a pursuit to encounter the Living God. He is waiting for you to display the knowledge of His glory in the earth. May the Gory Walker in you be revealed!

Chapter One

A Place of Dis-ease

I don't know if you have ever been in a place spiritually where there seems to be no escape. I am referring to a place of the greatest discontentment, discomfort and dissatisfaction I had ever experienced since accepting Christ as my Lord and Savior over twenty-three years ago. I arrived at this place because I had grown increasingly weary of the weekly Sunday show, and longed for an intentional, repeated encounter with the living God. You will see that I use the word dis-ease, not in the sense of a natural sickness in the body, but if I can say it, a sickness in my spirit. The sickness I am referring to is the discontentment I alluded to in the opening sentences of this chapter. As we begin this journey into my and soon to be your life changing encounter, I would advise you to find a comfortable spot and follow intently as I give an account of one of the most fascinating and humbling experiences of my life.

On the night of October 28, 2012 I experienced what I term as a sense of dis-ease in my spirit. I have been a believer for over twenty-three years, gone to church every Sunday, spoke in tongues, read my word daily, heard from God pretty well and served in leadership, but I was still discontent with my Christian life. As I sat reading my Bible that evening, I wondered why I/we were not seeing the demonstration of the power of the Holy Spirit as we read about in the book of Acts. Jesus said we would do the works He did and even greater works, **(John 14:12)**; but most of the works and definitely not the greater were nowhere in sight in my realm of influence. Granted, I had not just randomly arrived at this state; this was a feeling which haunted me all of 2012, but it came to a head on this particular night. I sat staring at my Bible wondering how men in the Old Testament could walk in greater revelation, power and demonstration of the Holy Spirit than New Testament believers who are filled with the Holy Spirit. How were they able to flow with God and gain instruction with such detail and accuracy? I felt a righteous indignation rise up on the inside of me because I knew as a New Testament believer that I was filled with the fullness of the Godhead, but my life compared to the Bible did not even closely resemble my Old Testament forefathers. This was equally the case when compared with the New Testament Apostles. I must admit, I was provoked to a point of jealousy and anger. I am not one given to tears, but this night I had to get out of my bed and go into the bathroom to keep from waking my husband because I was having a "moment." If you know what I am talking about, you know these kind of cries can get a bit out of hand. I had many more of these as the year came to a close.

It became quite evident that this feeling was not going to go away on its own. The more I thought about the great exploits done in Scripture the more incensed I became. Peter and Paul and so many New Testament disciples exhibited such great power and demonstrations for the kingdom, yet today the majority of believers have become satisfied with two fast songs, one slow song, reading the Bible only when it's seen on power point and a three point sermon. The thing which bothered me so much about church services was not the form but the lack of power. There was the missing link of the demonstration of the power of the Holy Spirit. So many pastors have become eloquent orators and storytellers who can preach at the drop of a hat. Many only look for a pat on the back from their congregants instead of the much needed confirmation from the Holy Spirit Himself. They/we have become preoccupied with the numbers rather than seeking the Lord, and assuring the bread God had for His people was delivered as instructed. For the most part this is what we have called church for as long as I can remember. I wondered how the body of Christ, and this includes me, had settled for goose bumps and programs, and dismissed the Holy Spirit from His services. What an awful thing to be kicked out of your own house by the very children you created! This appears to be the case on a broad scale. The Holy Spirit is being planned out of today's services. How grievous this must be to our Father.

How had I gotten to this place of dis-ease? I held on my lap and in my hands, a Bible loaded with power, yet I was not fully walking in this power. Now I will say, up to this point, I had laid hands on many people and seen them healed, and preached sermons where people's lives were changed, but I felt there was so much more to this life and life more abundantly which Jesus had promised me. I was driven to a point of desperation to encounter and demonstrate the presence of God on another level. May I add, until you find yourself in this place of desperation, what I am trying to articulate will remain a foreign language to you. Until normal is not enough for you, then the words on these pages won't mean very much; they will remain just that - words. I met with God and said, "I want this!" I wanted to walk in the same power as Jesus, Paul, Peter and some of those who boldly peeled back the lid and climbed out of the box of religion and tradition that most Christians find themselves in. I was and we are in this box because the divine design of the church has been reduced to a building and stripped of its power as a living body which serves as an extension of the hands, feet and mouth of Christ.

That night I made up my mind to never settle for church another day in my life! If I would have calculated all of the hours I was entertained with all kinds of programs and fillers, I probably would have sunk deeper into this place of dis-ease, but I would not permit myself to go any deeper. I wanted God, all of Him and I was not going to settle for anything less than a genuine encounter with Him every day! As you read through the progressing chapters you will see that God knew I meant business. I'm convinced He was patiently waiting to hear these words from me for a very long time. I believe the Godhead and all of heaven rejoiced to hear my words echo through the throne room of Heaven. Finally, Sonya L. Thompson had come to a place where she was going to die and really start living! You will understand this statement a little later. I read in my Bible, "**Those who seek the Lord lack no good thing (Psalm 34:10)."** Without a shadow of a doubt, I know this is the truth, because the Holy Spirit answered my plea of desperation as He dropped two words in my spirit, ***"Azusa Street."*** From that moment a fire began to kindle on the inside of me to learn more about this era in history. Little did I know it, but those two words would send me on a journey which *would* literally change the entire course of my life.

Chapter Two

What About Azusa Street?

I think I would be safe in saying that most Christians know about the Azusa street era. That's most Christians except for me. I had heard of the events of Azusa Street from a wonderful lady and now very close friend of mine by the name of Ms. Pat Hart. I knew great miracles had occurred during this moment in time, but I didn't know the details which led up to one of the most prolific outpourings of the demonstration of the glory of God.

Ms. Pat was always talking about and praying for the glory of God to come to our church. In our prayer circle, when she closed out our prayer time, she would passionately ask God to show and pour out His glory. Ms. Pat constantly reminded God of His promise to revisit us again with an outpouring of His glory. I had no issue with her prayers, but did not fully understand the longing in her to have the glory of God amongst us. I knew nothing of this type of experience she was continually asking for. I thought that what we had been experiencing up to this point was all we would ever encounter of the presence of God. We would have moments, glimpses, of what our experience was supposed to be; I call them hit or miss encounters with God, but never a full outpouring of His presence. It is a painful thing to think you have arrived and find out you are not even in the train station. As I type this chapter, my heart literally aches for the countless number of believers who gather each week and are convinced they have experienced the Living God, but have really had their ears tickled and their emotions stroked. They don't even realize that the lengthy programs and time fillers have crept in and taken the place of His presence. My friend, goosebumps and the church dance is not an indication of the presence of God. The flesh, human nature, is a funny thing; it does not take much to get it worked up. Please do not misunderstand me, I am not against dancing etc., but I am against a faux demonstration of the presence of God. I am against the deception of working people up emotionally in the guise of an encounter with God.

Well, it appeared Ms. Pat's prayers had been answered! After the Holy Spirit dropped *Azusa Street* in my heart, I immediately went online and began to gather as much information as I could about the Azusa Street revival. I stayed up until about four a.m., gathering every detail available about this time in our history. As I researched, I saw a link which led to an episode on the website of

Sid Roth. His guest was a very "normal" looking older man by the name of Brother Tommy Welchel, and he was talking about… yes, you know what, Azusa Street! He discussed how he had sat and talked with those who had actually participated in and been a part of the Azusa Street Revival! Tommy Welchel had been given the privilege of developing a relationship with and sitting with many of the participants as they told him their stories. Not only had he sat with them, but he eventually reached a point where each one laid hands on him and imparted their anointing to him as well. This won't mean very much to you unless you understand the importance of releasing the anointing through the law of contact and transfer. Impartation of the anointing is shown all throughout Scripture as a valuable experience for every believer. I increasingly see the enemy sneaking in and persuading pastors that the laying on of hands is no longer necessary. It may not be necessary in every instance but I assure you, if you can read your Bible, you know it is relevant and necessary to stir up the gifts and impart the anointing. Sorry for my digression. So, I ordered Brother Welchel's book, "They Told Me Their Stories," and the rest as you will soon realize, is history.

If God would have shown me then how the events of my life would evolve as a result of reading his book, I truly believe I would have put the brakes on at some point and settled for experiencing just a little more Jesus. This was the proverbial icing on the cake for me because it took me to a place of no return. After reading Brother Welchel's book I became consumed with experiencing the power of the Holy Spirit and seeing the glory of God to a greater degree. I was driven not only to just read the Bible but to **SEE** it every single day, in diverse places. I was tired of feeling like I was playing spiritual roulette where I/we pull the trigger and hope to experience a blast of the power of the Holy Spirit. Spiritual roulette is when we try to come up with the right song combination to bring His presence on the scene. It's time we come to realize that the formula for His glory is far more complicated than song selection and programs. But I will add this, the songs He selects will usher in the tangible presence of God. And you can only get this song list by asking Him exactly what He would like to hear.

I have moments in my life, pivotal moments, where a divine marker gets placed along my spiritual road and this was one of them. I equate the experience of hearing and researching the words Azusa Street, and reading, They Told Me Their Stories, to the day Paul was riding on the road to Damascus and was knocked off of his beast by the light of the glory of the Lord. It was a space in time where I realized for the last twenty plus years of my life, I had only scratched the surface of God's presence and power. I realized I really did not "know" the God of the Bible from the standpoint of His great power that was at work in me. It was a moment when I publicly announced, "I do not want church and will never do church again!" You may see this statement a few more times throughout this book. Hopefully by the time you finish reading, you will be saying these words as well. I still say it to this day as a reminder to myself that I will never go back to that thing they/we call church. My desire was and is to see people's lives impacted by the presence and power of the Living God. As I type this chapter I am reminded by the Holy Spirit of how Elijah threw his mantle over Elisha in I Kings nineteen. It was a call for Elisha to abandon all and to follow after the man of God, the prophet, who had a walk with God unparalleled by many. After the invitation, Elisha went back to his household, cut up his oxen and burned the carts he used to pull them. He left no room to go back to what was comfortable and convenient. Here was a man who abandoned his business and family for the anointing, presence and glory of God. This was how I felt, as if God had thrown His mantle over me and said, "Follow me, and abandon all for the greater glory I am going to show you." My answer was, is and will always be, "Here I am, Yes, I will follow you!"

I wanted a ministry marked by the extraordinary manifestation of the glory of God; A ministry where people's lives would forever be changed when they encountered the Living God of the Bible. Certainly God was not trying to get me to resurrect Azusa Street, though I have been accused of this, but He had some plans to use me in my region, to fulfill the promise He made to Brother Seymour to revisit His people in this mighty way again. I had no intention of being left out of this end time revival where the glory of God would no longer be poured out in one place, but over the entire earth. I decided I was going to walk in the same power of Christ as the Azusa street saints demonstrated and even greater. I decided I would, like Christ, be a glory walker and no one was ever going to put me back in a box again. Walking with and working with the Father was going to be the norm for me. Not only was I going to be a Glory Walker but I would allow the Father to employ me to raise up even more people like myself who were hungry and desperate for His presence, power and glory. Ah! Now I was moving into a place which I later discovered, would put me in a position of power with God. I continued to reread and talk about "They Told Me Their Stories" many more times, because I knew a moment would arrive where the supernatural would become the norm for my life and those around me. After all, I was panting after God, and He can't resist the cry of a desperate heart seeking after His presence!

Chapter Three

Panting and Thirsting
After God

I wish I could tell you things changed instantly for me, but they did not. I had read Brother Welchel's book, and got my hands on everything I could which related to the glory of God. I even watched videos online of ministers who flowed in the glory of God, but, it was not until the early summer of 2013 during Bible study where I would learn how to break out and break free. After I taught Bible study one Wednesday, a woman by the name of Ms. Dukes came to me and said she had a word from the Lord for me. I am paraphrasing what she said to me. She said, God knew I was discontent and that I was saying, "Surely there must be more." She told me the Lord said to go on a fast. I kept my poker face, because I was a minister, even though she had hit the nail on the head. "Surely there must be more," those were the very words I spoke to the Holy Spirit that morning during my prayer time! I hugged her and thanked her for being obedient to the Lord. As I rode home that night from Bible study, I said "Lord I can receive from whomever you send." As a side note, you don't have to have a title or degree to hear from God. All you have to do is make yourself available to Him. I told God, "If this is what you want me to do, I will fast." He then reminded me of all of the Scriptures He had sent me to that week which dealt with fasting! Isn't God so wonderful? Even when we don't get it, He sees to it that we get it. I always say, you can never make a mistake when you earnestly seek after God. He won't let it happen. I am convinced God can't resist the cry of a hungry and desperate heart. I decided I would begin a fast for the next few days and it would turn out that this pattern of fasting would continue for months and eventually become a permanent part of my life as a Glory Walker.

During the times of fasting, I noticed greater clarity in hearing the voice of God, understanding His word and the demonstrations of power had increased tremendously when I taught. I began to teach with a confidence which showed I had been with Jesus and it could not be denied. My words were alive and captivating because the breath of the Holy Spirit was upon them. On one occasion over twenty-eight people were filled with the Holy Spirit after I taught one Sunday morning. On occasions to follow I saw people delivered from demonic spirits and drug addiction. I began to operate in words of knowledge with great accuracy and clarity in the prophetic. It was overwhelming to say the least. It was what I had prayed and fasted for and for lack of a better word, it was scary! I mean scary in the sense of a reverent fear not an unhealthy fear. Who was this woman I had become? I did not recognize myself! I was in the flow, in awe of God, a little scared, but I knew there still had to be more! I have to admit, He had me hooked at this point, but I was still at dis-ease because I knew there was so much more. In **Psalm 42** David said, "**As the deer pants for the water brooks, So pants my soul for you Oh God."** I was the deer who was panting, longing and seeking after God. The deep of God's Spirit was calling out to the deep of my spirit and I could not, nor did I want to resist Him. For the first time in my Christian life I felt like I was no longer in control. Anyone who knows me intimately knows my personality. I like to be in control and keep things in order. Now there is a place for this, but not when you are seeking after God. All I can do is laugh because if being out of control is wrong, I do not want to be right. Little by little I had been drawn from a water level which was ankle deep, to knee deep, to waist deep then to a point where I was overtaken and consumed by the presence of God. If I can say it in a language you understand, I was in over my head! This happened without my being aware, until I was fully submerged under the water in the realm of the spirit.

This pattern of panting, praying and fasting continued for several months. Again, I watched remarkable things occur in my life and the lives of others during times of teaching. There were many instances when I would be having a casual conversation with someone and the Holy Spirit would speak a word of knowledge through me for that person. What amazed me was the accuracy of what I was saying. I would later gain revelation as to how men and woman of God can flow precisely in the prophetic realm. I felt like God was talking to me all of the time and this took some getting used to. I found myself having two conversations at one time, while trying to keep focused on the person speaking to me. It became very interesting when someone would tell me one thing and at the same time, the Holy Spirit would tell me that what they were saying was not true. He would show me the whole truth which they were not revealing to me. I did not feel compelled at that time to say anything, I just kept in my heart what He had shown me. On one occasion I went into a Walgreens store and as I stood behind a lady, the Holy Spirit told me she was a heavy drinker and He gave me her name, Kathy. I could not see what she had in her basket; it was loaded with so much stuff. But, from the bottom of the pile she pulled out not one, not two, but three very large bottles of wine. Then her mom came from another area of the store and called her by an abbreviated form of her name. She called her Kath! I was shaken to my core. After she checked out, I quickly paid for my items and literally ran to my car. What in the world was happening to me? This panting after God was getting very uncomfortable for me. His presence and voice had become so real to me. I found, and still find the very thought of Him provokes His presence to consume me and fill my atmosphere. If this was not enough, I began to experience open visions without warning. This still remains an amazing aspect of the supernatural to me. Our God can open up a scene right in the middle of whatever you are doing without warning and you are literally seeing into and experiencing situations in the realm of the spirit. I would have times where I had to excuse myself from conversations about Him, because His presence would come upon my whole body like a vibrating electricity. I literally felt His fire in my bones! My legs would become weak as my bones vibrated with such an intensity that I would have to take a seat to regroup. I had also come to a point where while I was asking He would answer me. I could go on, but I want you to understand what was happening to me was nothing short of amazing! I was panting after the Living God and every day He allowed me to drink the living water of His presence.

Many times, during corporate worship, I could sense the entrance of the King and I was compelled to go down on my knees and worship Him. I did not care about what other people thought about me. Those who knew me, knew this was not the norm for Sonya, because I just didn't play like that. Even my son asked me why I was always on my knees and if I cared about what other people thought. My response to him was, all I cared about was Him, honoring His presence and seeing His glory. I was long past the opinions of people. Was I uncomfortable? Yes and it was a wonderful place to be in. I could choose to remain in dis-ease or work through the uncomfortableness of being led and overtaken by the presence of the Living God. To me, the choice was quite obvious. Even with all of the great things I was experiencing, it did not quench my thirst. On the contrary, I was still compelled to pant after Him even more. I understand what Jesus meant when He said, **"man does not live by bread alone but by every word that proceeds from the mouth of the Father."** I longed for Him to speak and meet with me every single day. Where this new found hunger and thirst would take me was still a mystery to me, but I knew I was never going to go back to the way things used to be; that was NOT an option. The mechanics of "church" would never be an option for me again, so I decided to keep panting after Him.

We Are Not Alone

During this time of transition in my life, God sent a young lady to our church who led the worship team for a season. She is a phenomenal young lady who flows in the prophetic and knows how to appreciate and cultivate the presence of God. If ever there was anyone who has an ear in the realm of the spirit, who is sensitive to the movement of His presence and who could pick up on songs/sounds from Heaven, Shirmeka is one of them. When she opens her mouth, the presence of the Lord comes rushing into the atmosphere. This is an absolutely wonderful thing to witness. Shirmeka's private time with Him is always quickly validated in public. Though her voice is beautiful, it goes far beyond a beautiful voice. I felt as if God was singing through her to me and I could feel and pick up on the sound of Heaven.

After meeting and speaking in length with this young lady, I realized we were not alone! There was another and others who longed to encounter His presence. Sometimes you may feel like Elijah and believe you are the only one who is tired of the institution of religion and there is no one else left who is fighting for the just causes of God. Oh, I assure you there is a remnant in the earth which is passionately pursuing His presence. Shirmeka's passion is ministering to the Lord. When she ministers you sense that it's just her and God, and we just happen to get an opportunity to partake in their communion together. The overflow was and is always sweet and precious to me. Because she was used to create an atmosphere where the presence and glory of God filled the room, I became even more desperate to stay in this place with God. He also used her to reveal the connection between prophetic worship and the glory of God to me. And to top it all off, I later discovered Shirmeka had been earmarked before the foundation of the earth to become one of my spiritual daughters. What an absolute blessing she has been in my life and for this I am ever thankful to God!

Panting Is Contagious

Have you ever been with someone who is hungry and they spend so much time describing a delicious meal they are going to cook or buy and before you know it you find yourself hungry as well? Well, that's what began to happen to those around me. The way I described how "delicious" God was made them hungry too. Even David said to **"taste and see that the Lord is good."** Everyone knew something incredible had happened to me. When I spoke about God, His presence, His promises, His abilities, His power, His personality or anything directly related to Him, my words became alive. People began to feel the "weight" of my words, is how many have described it to me. They could literally sense the Holy Spirit's presence when I spoke because the very breath of God carried His fresh revelation to the hearts of the people. It kind of reminded me of the comment which was made about the disciples when Peter and John addressed the elders and rulers of Jerusalem.

Acts 4:13

Now when they saw the boldness of Peter and John, and perceived that they were uneducated and untrained men, they marveled. And they realized that they had been with Jesus.

With all humility I make the statements to follow. Many people marveled at what God was doing with and through me. Later on I found out there were many conversations concerning me, not all of which were good, but I will share one of the good ones before the close of this book. I had not attended seminary, no one pulled me to their side and tutored me, but the one thing which was evident to everyone is that I had been with Jesus. The Holy Spirit Himself had enlightened the eyes of my understanding and began to show me the Word; I am talking about Jesus, the Living Word, in a whole new way. He had become my teacher and as a result I was able to introduce others to a fresh encounter with the Living God.

I taught fresh revelation and it came across with great authority and power. God's stamp of approval was upon the messages and it could not be denied. I had a time when I had taught one of the most powerful messages of my life. It was a Sunday morning after I taught, the Holy Spirit had me make an altar call for those who wanted hands laid upon them to stir up the gifts. The altar was flooded! I had no clue the response would be so great. I also had no idea God would fill my mouth with accurate and precise words of knowledge and prophesy for so many people. This was remarkable and I gave God all of the glory. "Panters" were birthed that day. A desperation was birthed in the hearts of so many younger believers. It was overwhelming to witness. Then I realized, this thing was contagious!

A few days later during our mid-week service one of the associate pastors taught Bible study and he undermined me so He thought, but He really spoke against the Holy Spirit. In a very clever manner, he tried to discredit me in front of the congregation. I don't ever remember a time when I was so angry, not just for myself, but because He was trying to discredit the word God had given me for the body, even after so many people's lives had been changed. The spirit of religion and tradition always rises up when panters are birthed. This spirit longs to stifle and choke out the thirst for the Living God and replace it with vain and empty teaching. As a result of this experience the Bible began to take on a new reality to me. I saw that the enemy always comes to steal the Word when it is has been sown in the soil of the heart. I also found out Satan even uses pastors. Some people are not happy unless they are the focus of attention or the deliverer of revelation from God. Heaven forbid God use a woman to teach and operate in power! This was a very hurtful moment for me. I had always taken great care of not allowing anyone to wound me, but he had done it. I would recover after some time, but this was only the beginning of the persecution that was to come. It did not stop me personally, nor did it stop me from igniting the fire and passion of others. This experience only made me pant even harder after my Father.

Chapter Four

In Pursuit of His Glory

This new found reality and relationship with the Holy Spirit was wonderful. It seemed like I simply could not get enough time with Him. I was in pursuit of His glory. If I did not have a husband and son to take care of I can guarantee you I could have easily had a stretch of days where I stayed locked away talking to and communing with my Father. This next encounter I will describe occurred at the end of another lengthy season of fasting. It was approximately eight o'clock in the morning, and I was finishing up my prayer time. I had been studying on the different aspects of the glory of God. What was particularly intriguing was the account in Exodus thirty-three where God showed Moses His glory. If Moses could experience God in this manner, how much more for me, the New Testament believer?

I sat on my bed and began to pray in my heavenly language for a few minutes and something surreal happened. What I am about to share with you may be a little tough to believe, but I trust the Holy Spirit will confirm in your spirit that what I am sharing with you is the truth. The Holy Spirit told me Tommy Welchel was the last survivor who sat with and received an impartation from those who ministered during the *Azusa Street* era. The Lord told me to go to Arizona to receive this impartation. That's not all! Then, I was in a vision and I saw gates open up to a cemetery and Brother William Seymour was standing there with a Bible in His hand. Was this really happening? Yes, yes, yes! I jumped up from my bed and began to reason with God. I asked Him how was I going to get in touch with Brother Welchel? If I did, he probably was going to think I was nuts. Now we both know if God tells us to do something, the figuring out has already been done. Oh what an infinitely patient God we serve!

Finding Brother Welchel

After I gathered my mental bearings, I called my friend Ms. Pat and shared my encounter with her. This woman of God was ecstatic. Only a friend like this could hear something so surreal and not think I had lost my mind. We were on the brink of walking into the very "thing" she and I had prayed and fasted for. God had answered the cry of our hearts. After giving her an account of my experience with God, she said she was so happy God was sending me on this journey. I immediately said, "Me? You mean us!" There was no way I would go on this trip without Ms. Pat. The very reason all of this came about was because she was a lady who continued to cry out for the glory of God. With little coaxing, she agreed to accompany me. I had not even talked to Brother Welchel yet, but we were convinced we were going to see him because God had already spoken.

Right in the middle of this pursuit for His glory, let me take a moment to address something dear to my heart. When God uses other people to usher you into your divine destiny, don't forget about them. They are not your stepping stones. They should be someone you "go back" and get and take with you. This is a weakness in the body of Christ. Too many forget about the ones who helped them reach their destiny or those who are also anointed by God, and do not go back to help them reach their place of assignment. The example the Holy Spirit gave me was Joseph. There he sat in prison for years. In Genesis chapter forty, Pharaoh's chief butler and baker are thrown into prison with Joseph and both have a dream. God gave Joseph the interpretation of their dreams after which he makes this statement:

14 "But remember me when it is well with you, and please show kindness to me; make mention of me to Pharaoh, and get me out of this house. 15 For indeed I was stolen away from the land of the

Hebrews; and also I have done nothing here that they should put me into the dungeon."

Joseph sat in prison for two more years until Pharaoh had a dream which no one could interpret. In Genesis forty-one, the butler remembers Joseph interpreted his dream with accuracy. In a moment, Joseph went from being a prisoner to the Prime Minister. This is a lesson I intend to teach in my Bible studies and travels, "Don't Forget About Me." I say again, go back and help those who have helped you, whether it be financially, through prayer or even those who ministered alongside of you and have a unique calling and gifting from God. There is room for everybody's gifts and callings. Or should I say, there is room for God, because the gifts are His and the demonstration of them is evidence that He is amongst us. I could have forgotten about Ms. Pat and went on my journey, but there was no way to overlook the obvious: this woman of God was the catalyst to my change. She was coming with me in pursuit of His glory.

As we discussed how we could contact Brother Welchel, she remembered she had an older copy of His book and it actually had his phone number in it! My God, talk about this wonderful God we serve! She gave me the phone number, but I admit, I was not expecting to get him on the phone. I was sure a secretary would answer the phone on his behalf. I called Brother Welchel immediately after hanging up with Ms. Pat and to God be the glory, guess who answered the phone? Brother Tommy Welchel! I took a few moments to introduce myself to him. I began by saying, "I know you are going to think I'm crazy…" I told him what the Holy Spirit told me and showed me in a vision. This man of God said, "I do not think you are crazy, I know it is God. You know I am the last survivor right? So, when are you coming to Arizona?" I almost fell off the bed. Look at God! Here was a man who had never met me, but by the Spirit knew that God was all over this thing, for lack of a better word. Ms. Pat and I began to make plans to travel to Arizona; we wanted to go as soon as possible. After working out the details we settled on the date of December 16th of 2013.

I could not tell those close to me why I was going to Arizona, not even my own husband. I simply stated I had a ministry engagement there. My husband tried to inquire a little further, but I asked him to trust me. Plus, I told him Ms. Pat was accompanying me and this seemed to put him at ease. There are some things you can't disclose until the set time. Most people, including my husband would have thought this whole story was nuts. I could have just had him pray for me over the phone, right? Yes I could have **IF** that was what God told me to do, but it wasn't. It was easier for me to keep the details to a minimum because I knew the results would speak for themselves when we returned.

No Turning Back

Well the day arrived and here we were, a southern bell from Groveland, Florida and a young (I consider 46 at that time, young) black woman who is originally from New Jersey, on a journey to receive an impartation of this miracle working anointing. Imagine that! God could have chosen anyone else from this region, but He chose us. This assignment had been etched in eternity and had been ordained from before the foundation of the earth. You have no clue how humbling this was for both of us. To tell you that we could not contain ourselves would be an understatement. We were like giddy school girls because we knew this was a defining moment in our lives.

After we boarded our last flight heading into Arizona, Ms. Pat fell asleep and the Holy Spirit began to minister to me. In a moment I felt like God and I were the only ones on the plane; everything else began to fade. The sound of the air in the cabin was all I could hear as the Holy Spirit told me, "There is no turning back. You have no idea where this journey will take you, but I will be with you." Again, I was driven to tears. This moment gripped my heart, because a realization set in that I was on a journey which would be the door to my God given assignment and destiny. He said, "There is no turning back." I had no intention of doing so because this journey, this moment, the relationship the Holy Spirit and I had developed, meant everything to me! He had truly become my life. There was no way I was going to shrink back now. The very thing I had been asking for had been delivered. As His words settled in my mind and spirit, I was overwhelmed and I began to cry uncontrollably, but quietly. I didn't want Ms. Pat to see me crying, so I kept my face turned to the window, looking out into the night, still weeping. His words continued to resonate in me.

Over the course of the year and up to this moment, my relationship with the Holy Spirit had become so sweet, so real. The reality of God took on a new meaning for me. I didn't know it before, but He was always just a thought or word away. His attentiveness to me, my desires and difficulties was refreshing and filled me with such boldness, because my God was with me. I understood what David meant when he said in **Psalm 16:8, "I have set the LORD always before me: because he is at my right hand, I shall not be moved."** This journey had cost me more than anyone knew. It went well beyond the obvious twenty pounds I had lost; I had invested a great deal of time pursuing

His Glory. Therefore, I determined that nothing would ever make me turn back to the way it used to be. It was the Holy Spirit and myself from now on, so turning back was not an option!

Chapter Five

The Impartation

I called brother Welchel the morning after we had arrived in Arizona to let him know we were there and to set up a meeting time. He was excited to meet with Ms. Pat and myself. Ms. Pat, being the woman she is, knew from reading Brother Welchel's book, that he loved chocolate chip cookies and milk. She asked the hotel staff to provide milk and cookies for our guest and they happily accommodated her request. We waited in the hotel lobby for him, and there he was. We said our hellos and proceeded into the meeting room. Here was what most would consider a "normal" man from all accounts. He was rather tall, burly, in his sixties, maybe, and balding a bit. He looked like the average guy on the block. It's not my intention for this statement to be disrespectful at all, but to bring every believer to the stark reality that our Father does not look on the outside as men do, but on the heart. If you and I were to choose someone to carry this tremendous anointing, he would have looked totally different. Our Father chooses what we would consider foolish to confound the wise. Regardless of what he looked like, I could see and feel his humility. He was amused by the cookies and milk at the table. He drank the milk but said he would eat the cookies later. After getting acquainted for a bit, he began to tell us their stories.

The Great Story Teller

Ms. Pat and I sat in the hotel meeting room with great expectation. I told Brother Welchel to talk to us; we had come a long way and wanted to hear everything. He began to systematically recount the stories from his book. I have never in my life witnessed such an accurate accounting of details as this man delivered to us. We literally saw the book come alive as he described each participant from Azusa Street- how he met with them regularly and listened to their stories, and how they laid hands on him and imparted the anointing. Brother Welchel shared a little of his personal journey as a youth. He was something else before coming to Christ; as we all are. We sat for hours talking about Azusa Street and the different personalities of those involved. What I loved the most about his recollection of those visits, was the age of the participants. They were young and hungry for God. They dared to believe God could and would use them. No one cared about the age or title of the person ministering at Azusa Street, they just knew

God was there and He was working through everyone, young and old alike. This is what I longed for.

Just before we received the impartation of the anointing, Brother Welchel told us of one of the times Jesus appeared to Him in person when he was young. As he began to describe Jesus, especially His voice and the depth of His eyes, like liquid love, a heavy anointing and presence of God filled the room and I became undone. I began to weep because I could feel His presence in such a real way. I tried to compose myself but I couldn't. All I could see in my mind was the image of Jesus which Brother Welchel had so skillfully painted for us. God loves it when we talk about Jesus. He is drawn into an atmosphere where His Son is praised, honored and adored. Even now as I write this book, I am overwhelmed by the memory of this moment. The story teller had told us everything he knew and now it was time. First, Ms. Pat and I took out our seed offering. We had both prayed before the trip and asked the Holy Spirit to direct us on how much seed to sow into the life of this man of God. Now for my religious folks, no, we were not trying to buy the anointing. That seed was an extension of our faith and a seed to honor this man of God. I wrote a book called **"Seeds of Prosperity."** This book will give you more detail about this principle. Brother Welchel received my seed, laid hands on me and imparted the anointing. I was sitting and so was he. I thought I would mention this in case you thought you had to fall to receive an impartation. Ms. Pat and I traded chairs, she handed him her seed and then he imparted the anointing to her. We talked for a few minutes afterwards, then suddenly a heat began to move up my legs and then up my entire body. I looked at Ms. Pat and she started feeling the same thing. Ah, yes! Even though we didn't care whether we felt anything or not, God allowed us to feel the presence of the anointing. If I had felt nothing it would not have mattered to me at all. I know His voice and His voice is what caused us to travel from Florida to Arizona. His voice was all the evidence in which Ms. Pat and I needed to confirm the impartation of His anointing. But God! He allowed us the opportunity to feel what we had received and for this we were grateful.

We said our goodbyes, left Brother Welchel and went out for a quick dinner. If someone would have walked up and pinched us, it might have helped a bit. What are the chances of something like this happening to two ordinary people like us? This is so like God; He has a way of selecting the most unusually common people in the sight of man. The selection is not based on Him being a respecter or persons, but based on those who identify themselves as desperate and hungry for God. Our desperation and sacrifice to be close to Him was our qualification as far as God was concerned. And now we had to prepare for our journey back home; only God knew what we would encounter.

Don't Hoard the Oil

We boarded our plane early Wednesday morning, still in awe of God's favor and grace. Even to this day as I write this book, I am in awe of God's favor because I know He could have chosen someone else from my region, but He chose me. What a humbling thought. As we headed home, the Holy Spirit spoke very clearly in my spirit "Don't hoard the oil." In other words my/our mandate was to release this anointing as led by the Holy Spirit. Azusa Street was an outpouring limited to one area, but now God wanted to take that same anointing and spread it all over the earth. I am sure we are not the only people Brother Welchel has imparted this anointing to, but we are the only ones in this region and we took it very seriously. God had commissioned us to share what He had given us. It was time to see a return of the glory of God marked by miracles, signs and wonders and we were to be the catalyst in this region. It was time for the church to emerge as a people who would demonstrate the powerful Word of God on a global scale. Freely we had received, therefore freely we would pour into others. I imagine there are thousands of believers all over the earth crying out for the glory of God. A countless number looking at their Bible like I was, wondering where the demonstration of the Word was. Our Father has heard the cry of His people and now He has "come down" to answer the call. For this reason those words are still my driving force, "Don't hoard the oil." It is like fire shut up in my bones. Where does one go when the fire is on the inside? At least in the natural if we touch something hot, we can pull our hand away from the fire for relief. But, when the fire is on the inside, there is no pulling away, there is no immediate relief! I am driven by this mandate. My relief comes only when I pour out the precious oil of His anointing through teaching and the laying on of hands, as directed by His Spirit.

The downfall of some of the greatest men and women in the body of Christ has been the spirit of pride. It is the fastest way down. In **Luke 10:18,** Jesus said, **"I saw Satan fall like lightening from heaven."** Whenever we try to own what belongs to God and steal His spotlight and glory, the only safe direction for us is down. I determined I would not be one of pride's victims. I remind myself daily that this is God's anointing, not mine and its purpose is to manifest His presence, character and nature to His people. The anointing is not given to draw attention to us but to Him. For many, this has proven to be a very difficult hurdle to overcome because there is an inherent nature in the flesh to be the center of attention. Our sinful nature loves to have its ego stroked. Imparting the anointing is the greatest defense against pride. So with this in mind I say, "Yes Father, I promise you, I will not hoard the oil."

Chapter Six

Walking With God- The Consuming Fire

We returned from our trip refreshed and renewed, with great expectation to see the manifestation of the glory of the Lord. I can't remember a time when the presence of God felt so real to me. **Acts 17:28** became my ever present reality. In Him I lived, moved and had my very being. This verse of Scripture is a snapshot of the glory cloud from the book of Exodus. The children of Israel were taught to exist in a way where they never moved without the presence of God leading them. When the cloud moved, they moved and when the cloud stayed still they did the same. So, what does this look like as we walk with God- the consuming fire? **In Him we live**: In Him we have true life, gain power, experience the living water; are vigorous and full of life. **In Him we move**: we are set in motion by His Spirit alone, with a motion which proves He is in us. In other words, people should see and feel the life of God when we are in motion. **In Him we have our being:** Our very existence is in Him. When people see you, I am making it personal now, they see Christ. If I were to put this into a few impactful sentences it would be as follows: When you walk with God, the living water, true life will flow through you to others. When you are in God motion, you will invade the atmosphere of others to a point where they collide with the glory of God. Your consummation by His presence will inevitably draw others in as well.

There is absolutely nothing more important to me than walking with God - the consuming fire, every minute of every hour of every day. This walk came as a result of my being convinced that this relationship surely had the potential to supersede just being an experience and become MY ever present reality. Most people think that it's not possible to walk with God on this level and many believe the awareness of His presence can only be felt or experienced in a church building. There is nothing spooky about walking with our God, the all - consuming fire. My friend you are the church and when you enter the building it should be profoundly evident that you are a Glory Walker. It should be without question that you have been with Him. Your private experience with our Father should burst forth and create an atmosphere pregnant for healing, deliverance, words of knowledge, songs from heaven and so forth.

For where the spirit of the Lord is, there is liberty-2 Corinthians 3:17.

Walking with God is far from a common, ordinary relationship. Jeremiah spoke of the Word of God like a fire shut up in his bones.

Jeremiah 20: 9

Then I said, I will not make mention of him, nor speak any more in his name. But *his word* was in mine heart as a burning fire shut up in my bones, and I was weary with forbearing, and I could not *stay*.

If I could express this in more vivid terms, God Himself creates such a pressure and boiling in us which drives and compels us to let Him out. It is similar to having a pressure cooker within. This is the only way I can describe what I began to feel. At one point I had literally come to a place of depression, because I needed to express this burning in me. As stated previously, in the natural when one touches fire, the normal reaction is to withdraw from its heat. But how do you escape the internal, consuming fire of God? Once you recognize the reality of Him, where can you go from His presence? The only spiritual expression of getting away from the consuming fire of God within, is to release it into the atmosphere through the inspired Word and by the demonstration of the same signs and wonders that Jesus walked in.

I'm convinced His abiding presence must be expressed. Our Father wants to burst forth into the atmosphere, so that His nature and character may be revealed across the nations. Our purpose is to fill this earth with the knowledge of the glory of the Lord as the waters cover the sea **(Habakkuk 2:14)**. Walking with God and displaying His glory - His manifested presence goes hand in hand. We can't have one without the other. Knowledge of the glory must be seen. No longer can we have men and women in the pulpits across the nation delivering carefully orchestrated speeches on Sunday mornings, where they look for the shouts of men, the clapping of hands and standing of the congregation to confirm their whimsical phraseology and expressions. Though there is nothing wrong with any of this, but many times the crowd is pumped to a place where these expressions are merely fill-ins for the obvious absence of the presence of the anointing. The flesh is easily manipulated when the senses are appealed to, making one think they have had a genuine encounter with a Living God. Just because you feel good does not mean the anointing was present. Dear friends, noise does not equal the anointing. Clamor will never replace the presence of the Holy God and the true demonstration of the signs which accompany His Word. No! We need a body of preachers, ministers, teachers and believers who intentionally and evidently walk with the Living God. Let's look at 2 Corinthians chapter three for a moment

2 Corinthians 3:6

Who also made us sufficient as ministers of the new covenant, not of the letter but of the Spirit; <u>for the letter kills, but the Spirit gives life</u>.

The letter without the Sprit is dead. A book report does not change the lives of the people. Three bullet points and beautifully designed power point images can't change lives. Quoting Scriptures is not evidence of spiritual power. The Pharisees, Scribes and teachers of the law in Jesus' days were experts in quoting Scriptures. Only the fresh breath of God can revive that which is dead or dying. The Spirit given life has to be seen. If the breath of the Holy Spirit is not on the Word, then life is not being released. When the inspired God breathed word goes forth, miracles happen and people's lives change because God watches over His Word to perform it. Paul said we are to be living epistles read by men.

2 Corinthians 3:2-3

2 You are our epistle written in our hearts, known and read by all men; 3 clearly you are an epistle of

Christ, ministered by us, written not with ink but by the Spirit of the living God, not on tablets of stone but on tablets of flesh, that is, of the heart.

This is what a Glory Walker looks like. He is an obvious, outright display of the Living God. A Glory Walker is Jesus, the Living Word of God in action. Jesus said in **John 14:9** *"He who has seen me has seen the Father."* My question for you is, have they seen Him through your life, through your words, and through your hands?

Disappearing In His Presence

John the Baptist understood the assignment of the Glory Walker. His assignment and instruction was to disappear. If I can say it more directly, the Glory Walker's assignment is to die. When you step into His consuming fire, the only option is death. In **John 3:3** when Jesus appeared on the scene, John understood it was time for him to decrease and for Jesus to increase. It's human but not spiritual nature to desire to stay in the front. There is this desire in us to be seen by and affirmed by men. Many times we try to own what we have been given stewardship over. Our gifts are not ours, they are given to us to put God on display. As Glory Walkers we must move with the timing and seasons of God. This means we must be prepared to shift and change position as the Spirit wills. John understood this dynamic clearly and did not try to hold on to his position and place of prominence; he was comfortable with his new assignment to decrease. When we truly take on the assignment of the Glory Walker we embrace the necessity of disappearing/ dying in His presence, so that His nature and character are in the forefront of our lives. The Bible presents this dynamic in a very profound way. Paul writes,

Galatians 2:20

I have been crucified with Christ; it is no longer I who live, but Christ lives in me; and the life which I now live in the flesh I live by faith in the Son of God, who loved me and gave Himself for me.

A Glory Walker should have been assigned the phrase *"dead man walking,"* instead of those headed to execution. Based on Paul's animated description of the lifeless believer, I am sure you would agree. I realize my use of this example might be a bit unsettling to some and unless you have missed it, that is the main objective of this book from the beginning until the final page, to produce an unsettling and dis-eased feeling deep within you. Until you reach a place of permanent death, the term Glory Walker will only be another catch phrase for you and not a lifestyle you will excel to. If your desire is to be seen and recognized by men, then you have already forfeited the title and assignment. Let's be honest, we both know, being dead isn't really a popular place for the *average* Christian. Pastors, singers and believers who seek notoriety, popularity and the approval of men will never attain to the high calling of a Glory Walker, because dead men are covered by dirt and put out of sight. There are no spotlights or applause in the grave and dead bodies no longer have any feeling. To impress this even further, nobody in their right mind wants to keep a dead body on display for longer than necessary! We go through the natural process of preparing the body of those who exit this life by embalming and burial because dead things eventually stink and need to be covered up. So it is with us, when we want to leave our dead body in the forefront and shine more than Christ, a stench goes before us everywhere we go. From a natural standpoint, one can appear to be the best teacher, preacher, worship leader, usher etc., but from a heavenly perspective, their service is the stench of a dead body to the Father, because they refuse to be laid to rest. The only sweet aroma to Him is that of His Son. The only sweet aroma to the Consuming Fire is the aroma of a dead sacrifice.

Those who fall in love with self- the dead body, and the attention God's gift brings them more than the glory which should be ascribed to His name in this earth, will never willingly consent to being laid to rest. It usually takes drastic circumstances for believers to willingly turn loose of their dead body. But the Glory Walker embraces this death/life conversion Paul speaks about. The need to be clothed in Christ becomes overwhelmingly necessary for the Glory Walker and he/she welcomes death. Why? Because we know He is our burial cloth and tomb. My God that got me excited! Being clothed in Christ assures YOU are covered up and "put away" properly, never to rise again; and Christ who lives in you will emerge. You have the privilege to walk with the Living God at all times and to be ever aware of His holy presence. The exchange is death for life.

On a side note, in Genesis chapter five, even Enoch who was not filled with the Holy Spirit walked with God until he was literally caught up by Him; He disappeared from the earth. So this state of non-existence should be easy for the New Testament believer since we are filled with His Spirit right?

This new life or should I say *"death"* is so far from what I had experienced most of my Christian existence. When I decided it was OK to lay Sonya L. Thompson to rest, then Christ was able to emerge from the tomb of my life. As I write this book, I feel like Joshua did after he endured the wilderness and finally stepped into the promised-land after 40 years of "stuff." I have also made my journey through the wilderness, fought long and hard, and I now have my inheritance – HIM, my exceeding great reward. He is my everything! After all of these years of being a Christian, I discovered what it means to enter His rest. All I had to do was disappear by allowing the fire of His presence to consume me. It's a place where I walk in the spirit every minute of the day and am keenly aware of His indwelling and surrounding presence. I am keenly aware that Sonya L. Thompson is a dead man walking. This my brother and sister is a beautiful place to be in. He has also reserved a spot on the altar of sacrifice just for you.

Chapter Seven

Abiding In His Presence

Once you come to grips with your death, there is this beautiful place of rest you will enter into. It's called a place of abiding. Let's look at Jesus' description of what exemplifies the life of an abider.

John 15:1-8

"I am the true vine, and My Father is the vinedresser. 2 Every branch in Me that does not bear fruit He takes away; and every branch that bears fruit He prunes, that it may bear more fruit. 3 You are already clean because of the word which I have spoken to you. 4 <u>Abide</u> in Me, and I in you. As the branch cannot bear fruit of itself, unless it abides in the vine, neither can you, unless you abide in Me. 5 I am the vine, you are the branches. He who abides in Me, and I in him, bears much fruit; for without Me you can do nothing. 6 If anyone does not abide in Me, he is cast out as a branch and is withered; and they gather them and throw them into the fire, and they are burned. 7 If you <u>abide</u> in Me, and My words <u>abide</u> in you, you will

ask what you desire, and it shall be done for you. 8 By this My Father is glorified, that you bear much fruit; so you will be My disciples."

The subject matter of abiding is so vast that I would have to write another book about it, only then to realize I have just scratched the surface of it. But this aspect of being a Glory Walker can't be neglected, since it's the cornerstone to your relationship with the Father and produces the outward display of and manifestation of His presence. I venture to say someone who claims to be a Glory Walker and does not abide in Him and He in them, is merely a visitor. David said,

"One thing have I desired of the Lord, that will I seek after; that I may dwell in the house of the Lord all the days of my life, to behold the beauty of the Lord, and to enquire in his temple (Psalm 27:4 KJV)."

David truly understood the purpose of being an abider. He knew dwelling in the presence of God was more than goose bumps, a shake, shout or carefully choreographed Holy Ghost dance.

Dwell as used in this text means to sit down with, to remain, to set, to cause to sit, to cause to abide. With this knowledge in mind, let me paraphrase this text for you. David was saying, God, my desire is to just find a way to get right in your face or so close to the beauty of your presence, that you invite me to sit down/dwell with you, because you can see by my pursuit of you, that it's my one and only desire. If I can just get into that position, I am going to stay there forever. My God! May we have the mind and heart of David to know that abiding with God is all we will ever need.

We like to quote *Isaiah 54:17* when trouble rises against us, **"no weapon formed against you shall prosper."** But if the truth be told, there are a whole lot of formed weapons prospering against Christians who are quoting this very Scripture. Was God playing a trick on us here or what? Now let me let you in on a little secret, this is only true of the abider because He is sitting in God's face twenty-four hours per day. There is no way God is going to let anything or anyone sneak up on you when your only desire is being with Him! Weapons are prospering against our regular Christian folk because they don't have time to spend with Him, read His Word or listen for His instruction. But, they do have time to get dressed up and go to the building we mistakenly call the church, and allow themselves to believe this is the essence of abiding. The one who relies on moving from one position in the physical to another to see, hear and experience God is merely a visitor.

Psalm 91:1

He who _dwells_ in the secret place of the Most High Shall abide under the shadow of the Almighty.

I think I just saw that word dwell again. If you spend time reading this text in full, you will quickly notice the protections afforded to the abider. Notice the boldness of the abider. He decrees and declares… I will say of the Lord He is, and God responds because He has set his love on Him.

14 "Because he has set his love upon Me, therefore I will deliver him; I will set him on high, because he has known My name. 15 He shall call upon Me, and I will answer him; I will be with him in trouble; I will deliver him and honor him. 16 With long life I will satisfy him, And show him My salvation."

The promises above are only for the Christians who make the presence of God a permanent place of residence.

The Branch and the Vine

Jesus gives us a phenomenal example of the abiding relationship through the imagery of the connection between a branch and a vine. To keep it simple, abiding with God in the Greek means to tarry, to continue to be present, to be held in a place, kept, continually, to remain as one and not to become different.

Abiding goes far deeper than a confession of Jesus as Lord and Savior. If you abide in Him, you are increasingly aware of your inefficiency outside of Christ. You recognize that your daily connection to Him, not just your confession of Him, is essential to your very existence. Jesus made it clear that the one who is not intimately and intricately connected to Him as their life source can't bear fruit. I should say, they can't bear **God's** fruit. We are all connected to something or someone. Therefore, the connections you maintain will produce fruit of its own kind. Abiding requires that you remain the same and do not become different. So it is when we are connected to or abiding in Christ, our fruit will be consistent, not different from the life source we are drawing from. As an abider, the task of staying in place is solely up to you. Jesus, who is the vine, is unchanging. He is the same yesterday, today and forever. So, if He is unchanging, then this means the only one who has the possibility of moving out of position is you, the branch.

There's a simple truth about branches, they can be cut off from the life source but still look like they are alive. But, if you check back after a few days it has withered and died. This process of dying happens subtly, a little at a time, until eventually it's too late to recover. This is what happens to many believers who do not cultivate a relationship of abiding with Christ. Their hallelujahs, shouting, dancing and clapping give the external appearance of a connection, but in the spirit, they are disconnected, withering and dying daily. They are branches who are no longer connected to the vine.

The price for abiding is your time. It is the currency to occupy this position. You literally trade time for His presence. Nobody wants to wait on God anymore. We live in a microwave society and expect to push a button and see a mighty move of God in 10-15 minutes. Listen, I speak to you from the vantage point of living in this reality. You must be willing to abandon everything to become a Glory Walker. The one thing we cheat on when it comes to the presence of God is time. Even when we meet together as believers, so many pastors apologize for the time when the Holy Spirit moves. Do NOT make apologies for God. When the presence of God is in the atmosphere I can assure you nobody wants to leave. There are also men/women of God who fill the meetings with programs and unnecessary conversation and do not care about your time, nor do they apologize for stealing it. If you are a pastor, don't you ever apologize when there is a genuine move of the Holy Spirit! The apology should be made by the former group. As a matter of fact, Jesus NEVER apologized for His lengthy sermons which were accompanied by the demonstration of His power. He ministered so effectively and with such a heavy anointing, that at one point the people had not eaten for days! My God, try that today and you will be in a whole lot of trouble!

If time is your god, you can stop reading now; there is no way to effectively abide with God if time is your treasure. We tend to make time for whatever is important to us. I hear a lot of people say they just don't have time to pray and read the Word, but they are on social media several hours per day. Why? Because that is what's important to them and they enjoy the instant gratification of page likes and comments. Let's look at **John 15** again - verses **7 & 8** for a moment.

7 If you <u>abide</u> in Me, and My words <u>abide</u> in you, you will ask what you desire, and it shall be done for you. 8 By this My Father is glorified, that you bear much fruit; so you will be My disciples."

Reading and studying the Word of God keeps you connected to the vine. He said if my WORDS abide in you. How does the Word of God get to a place of abiding – to tarry, to continue to be present, to be held in a place, kept, continually, to remain as one and not to become different in one's life? Very simply, by reading and meditating on the Word and asking the Holy Spirit to teach you. Ask Him to uncover and reveal the hidden truths of the Word. When you get to this stage, notice Jesus says then and only then can you ask what you desire and it shall be done. When the abiding Word is with you and in you, your desires will be right and consistent with the nature and character of the Living God. This is where the God fruit comes in. Perhaps this is the main reason why as a body of believers, we are barren in the area of bearing much fruit.

Maybe this is why we are asking and not seeing, because we are not abiding in His presence and in His Word. Perhaps we are like the lifeless, disconnected branches laying along the roadside. We are going to church but the masses never open their Word to confirm what they have been taught. We simply say amen to every fancy phrase that tickles our ears and ignites our emotions. Nor do we search the Scriptures to uncover fresh revelation from Heaven. If we fail in these areas, our Father can't be glorified because there will be no manifestation of God fruit in our lives. I am not just talking about the fruit of the Spirit, love joy patience, etc. I am also referring to the fruit of blind eyes being opened, the lame walking, the deaf hearing, the captive being set free and the dead being raised to life again. Doing the works of Jesus requires people who are willing to stay connected to the vine. The fruit is our proof of daily being in His presence.

The Two Become One Flesh-
Forsaking All Others

When we hear the terms, the two become one flesh and forsaking all others, the first thing that comes to mind is the marriage vow between a man and a woman. The Bible says a man leaves His father and mother and cleaves to His wife. In other words, he forsakes everything and everyone to protect the value of the marriage covenant. In the spirit, the husband and wife are literally stuck together and inseparable! Many times when couples have been married for a while they actually start to look like one another. When they speak, the other is able to complete the sentence, because they are walking in unity as one flesh. This is the way our relationship should be with our Father. I am convinced if we understand the spiritual marriage with our Father through Christ Jesus, there will be less Christian divorces across the nation. I thought I would just throw that in as a freebie.

Though this use of the marriage vow is absolutely correct, the first real marriage vow we make is when we enter into a marriage covenant with Christ by publicly confessing Him as our Lord and Savior. Our Father paralleled the natural institution of marriage alongside the spiritual institution of marriage to Him. So if I can express this a little clearer in case you missed it, the natural marriage vow is an outward reflection and display of what we experience with the Father through Christ Jesus. Just as married couples begin to look alike and complete each other's sentences, it should be the same in the spirit. I should look like Jesus and talk like Him. As part of abiding with the Living God, we must be willing to put every other agenda and person aside to cleave to Him alone. Everything and everyone else comes after your commitment to Him. If anything or anyone jeopardizes your place with your Father, then they/it must be released. I know this sounds very cold and hard, but it's necessary if you want to abide with/in God and have Him abide with/in you. The two, you and God, must become one flesh. That's the nature of abiding. When they see you, they see God. When you speak, they hear God. When you touch, they feel the Master's touch. When you step into the room, His presence should be felt. Leaving and cleaving- forsaking all others for Him is the mark of an abider.

Chapter Eight

Throne Room Conversations

I have always been pretty open with others when it comes to hearing from God. Since this divine encounter, my clarity and accuracy of hearing has been taken to another level. One thing I have learned is that God talks, and He talks all of the time to whomever has ears to hear. I once had a pastor take a "low blow" at me from the pulpit, because I was open about the things the Lord was speaking to me. He said, "Watch out for people who are always talking about hearing from God. God does not talk that much!" I beg to differ! Evidently he had not been reading his Bible. We serve a God who longs to share His plans and thoughts with His children. The Bible is loaded with throne room conversations; God is simply looking for someone He can share His heart with. He is on the lookout for a Glory Walker who will pick up on throne room conversations and begin to decree and declare what He says. The comment by this pastor came as result of his own inability to hear with clarity. Maybe I should say, his inability to take the time to cultivate a relationship which would make him privy to the same throne room conversations I was participating in. It's a funny thing about religious/prideful people, if it's not happening through them or if the attention is not directed to them, they'll try to find a way to quiet down or discredit the one who is experiencing God on another level.

We find an account of this in the book of **Acts chapter 5:15-18**

15 so that they brought the sick out into the streets and laid them on beds and couches, that at least the shadow of Peter passing by might fall on some of them. 16 Also a multitude gathered from the surrounding cities to Jerusalem, bringing sick people and those who were tormented by unclean spirits, and they were all healed. 17 Then the high priest rose up, and all those who were with him (which is the sect of the Sadducees), and they were filled with indignation, 18 and laid their hands on the apostles and put them in the common prison.

In this reference the root of offense which caused the high priest (pastor) to rise up against Peter was envy and jealousy; so much so that the healings were totally ignored! This is how I liken the ill comments which were made by the pastor I mentioned. I would place him in this same category. It's a very dangerous thing to speak against someone who stays in the face of God and makes themselves available for throne room conversations. Notice I didn't say, it's dangerous just to speak against a pastor. The qualification here is the one who makes him or herself available to God. Whenever demonstrations of the glory of God are manifested, the heart of the witnesses will be revealed. The spirit of tradition and religion is cloaked by envy, pride and jealousy, but tends to draw attention to another area to prevent the real offense from being uncovered. The issue in the personal example I shared was that God was using me as a vessel to heal, deliver and set His people free. So, what better way to try and discredit me than to question my ability to hear? This was merely an attempt to get the people to overlook the obvious demonstrations of His power!

I shared this statement in a lesson I taught about hearing from God: "It's abnormal **NOT** to hear from God!" If you are His child, then you should be talking to and hearing from Him several times per day. The norm is to hear from God! I would be very concerned if He stops speaking. Don't let anyone discourage you when it comes to hearing Him. Jesus is talking; the question is are you listening? Let me caution you concerning a very important aspect of hearing from God. Don't ever become so comfortable with Him that you don't test the spirits by the Spirit. The devil talks too and he is very cunning and subtle. He knows how to twist the truth into a lie and pair it with that age old statement, did God really say or is he/she the only one who can hear from God? He is a master at getting you to come against and question those in authority or those being used by God.

Aaron and Miriam were guilty of this sin.

Numbers 12: 1-2

Then Miriam and Aaron spoke against Moses because of the Ethiopian woman whom he had married; for he had married an Ethiopian woman. 2 So they said, "Has the Lord indeed spoken only through Moses? Has He not spoken through us also?" And the Lord heard it.

The real issue was not whether Moses was hearing from God. The root of their offense was Moses' Ethiopian wife. I caution you not to allow the enemy to use you to come against those in authority, it will hinder your walk with the Lord. He will cause you to focus on an absolutely unimportant aspect of that man or woman of God in an effort to disconnect you from your place of provision and blessing. Don't allow the enemy to cause you to speak against those whom God has assigned in your life. If you follow this account through, Miriam ended up with leprosy and if it were not for Moses' intercession for her, she would have been destroyed.

Another safeguard is to always try and balance what you hear in relation to His Word. I must also make you aware that many times God will speak or give instructions where you can't find a Scripture to reference. For example, one time I prayed for a lady who had torn tissue in her calf. She had consulted with her physician and was going to have to schedule surgery. My spiritual daughters and I laid hands on her and spoke to her calf. She said she felt better, but I could tell she was still limping a bit. That did not sit well in my spirit. I had to run an errand and during the trip, I asked the Lord what we had missed because everyone He touched was always healed completely. He told me she had one sore spot on her calf and showed me where it was. He also told me when I touched it to speak to the calf and command a "divine suture" to come into place. This is not an instruction I could find in the Bible! I had no reference of a divine suture anywhere from Genesis to Revelation. When I got back to the office I asked her to come and see me. I took my hand and touched the spot the Lord had shown me and she acknowledged that was where the soreness was. I spoke exactly what the Lord told me to and she was instantly healed! As a result of what happened to her, her fiancé came to church that Sunday and the Lord used me to give him a word of knowledge. This man fell to the floor under the power of the Holy Spirit, then got up and received Jesus as His Savior. None of this would have ever happened had I not made myself available to hear a throne room conversation concerning this woman! This is why it's so important to sit in on those throne room conversations to tune your ear to His voice. These conversations put you on a level to minister to the people of God with effectiveness and accuracy.

Chapter Nine

Your Throne Room Conversations

There is a term in stock trading called insider trading. It is generally associated with an illegal aspect, though this is only partially true. There are also legal conditions which apply to insider trading. If we look at the illegal side of this practice, those involved as traders on the stock exchange can find themselves in a whole lot of trouble if they give out insider information or "tip" clients on trades. As a Glory Walker, throne room conversations with the Living God put you in a position to receive insider information without the legal repercussions. You get the privilege of being "tipped" on current and future events from the Living God. Isn't our God awesome? These are conversations within the Godhead which have been reserved just for you. They are directly connected to your daily assignment, destiny and the lives of others. These conversations also birth revelation and insight in the Word and allow you to see and experience the multifaceted nature and glory of our amazing God.

A Glory Walker has been given the privilege, authority and the power to operate seamlessly in two places at one time. I call this the unfair, yet fair advantage. It's fair because it's part of your inheritance through Christ Jesus. It's unfair because you have an ear in the spiritual realm, and you are able to thwart or prepare for every demonic attack and trap the enemy lays out for you. You also receive insider information in the areas mentioned above. One morning, the Holy Spirit impressed in my spirit a few verses of Scripture to give me greater clarity.

Hebrews 4:16

Let us therefore come boldly to the <u>throne of grace</u>, that we may obtain mercy and find grace to help in time of need.

Ephesians 2:5-7

5 even when we were dead in trespasses, made us alive together with Christ (by grace you have been saved), 6 and raised us up together, <u>and made us sit together in the heavenly places in Christ Jesus</u>, 7 that in the ages to come He might show the exceeding riches of His grace in His kindness toward us in Christ Jesus.

In the Scripture reference above, the throne of grace is Jesus Himself. It's not a seat, it's a person. Grace comes upon anything He touches. And we can go boldly before Him to hear throne room conversations for whatever that time of need may be. What an awesome privilege! Then we see in Ephesians, the aspect of sitting in heavenly places. This literally means you operate from another level of authority. You have a foot in the earth and at the same time your head and ears are in the throne room of Heaven. My God, how can we lose with an advantage like this? That's why you can't focus on the things of this earth. You clearly have the upper hand. You have been given everything that pertains to life and godliness (**2 Peter 1:3**).

Jesus, a Glory Walker, showed us how to effortlessly transition from the spirit to the natural every day. The secret was meeting with the Father every morning and talking to Him. You thought the secret was deep and profound didn't you? Your time, your ear and your obedience is what is required. If you want to partake in throne room conversations, then you must decide to passionately pursue His presence daily. You must determine to sit at His feet with an ear to hear and the willingness to obey.

Here is an example of what a throne room conversation looks like:

2 Kings 6:8-12

8 Now the king of Syria was making war against Israel; and he consulted with his servants, saying, "My camp will be in such and such a place." 9 And the man of God sent to the king of Israel, saying, "Beware that you do not pass this place, for the Syrians are coming down there." 10 Then the king of Israel sent someone to the place of which the man of God had told him. Thus he warned him, and he was watchful there, not just once or twice. 11 Therefore the heart of the king of Syria was greatly troubled by this thing; and he called his servants and said to them, "Will you not show me which of us is for the king of Israel?" 12 And one of his servants said, "None, my lord, O king; but Elisha, the prophet who is in Israel, tells the king of Israel the words that you speak in your bedroom."

While the enemy was planning the destruction of the King of Israel, Elijah, a Glory Walker, had his ear in the realm of the spirit and picked up on a throne room conversation which would preserve the nation. Now you should have greater revelation of the Scripture that says, **"if God is for us, who can be against us (Romans 8:31)."** No one can plan your demise when you are privy to throne room conversations. God will ensure your ear is literally in their bedroom!

On many occasions I have experienced this first hand. One time the Lord gave me an open vision of a meeting some of my church leadership had concerning me. People were getting nervous because of the way the Lord was using me to manifest His presence. Because I understand the concept of being in two places at one time, I was allowed to sit in on their meeting without being there physically! From that time on, God allowed His Spirit to show me every move they made by giving me a word of knowledge, a dream or a vision. Truly, I had the upper hand. As their plan unfolded, though it was still hurtful, I was not surprised or caught off guard when it manifested. When you make a conscious effort to sit in on your throne room conversations, it's impossible for any formed weapon to prosper against you!

Conversations – The Release of His Glory

Throne room conversations put you in a position to obtain crystal clear instructions for your daily assignments. They will involve those connected to you, and those you will encounter by divine assignment. If you want to be used by God to display and release His glory in the earth, you must come up higher to hear a throne room conversation.

The glory of God is the manifest presence of God. This manifestation comes in the form of deliverance, healing, words of knowledge, the cloud etc. When the glory of God shows up everything is accelerated and flows with ease. Something must happen when the glory of God shows up. We should never just sit and enjoy the glory of God without some form of manifestation occurring. God wants to touch His people. Therefore, when His glory manifests, we have to listen to find out what He wants to break out at that moment, then we can respond accordingly. A demonstration of the power of God is a necessary result when the glory of God shows up, otherwise we have only had a good feeling. The glory manifests to change, rearrange, dismantle and restore people's lives and situations. As a Glory Walker you have been commissioned to release His presence, character and nature in the earth through your hands, feet and mouth. The only way this world will experience the manifested presence of the Lord Jesus Christ is through you. This world, like Phillip, is crying out, **"Show me the Father."**

So how does one move in this dynamic realm of the spirit? Jesus showed us how to receive insider information that releases the glory of God; He only said and did what He heard and saw the Father doing.

John 12:49-50

49 For I have not spoken on My own authority; but the Father who sent Me gave Me a command, what I should say and what I should speak. 50 And I know that His command is everlasting life. _Therefore, whatever I speak, just as the Father has told Me, so I speak_."

John 5:19-20

19 Then Jesus answered and said to them, "Most assuredly, _I say to you, the Son can do nothing of Himself, but what He sees the Father do; for whatever He does, the Son also does in like manner._ 20 For the Father loves the Son, and shows Him all things that He Himself does; and He will show Him greater works than these, that you may marvel.

The two references above are a lesson on how to release the glory of God with a demonstration of His power every single time. He simply said and did whatever the Father instructed Him to do. You step into a Glory Walker Revealed status when you hear and do what the Lord desires. When my spiritual daughter and I pray for people at our church or in our travels, we get results! People are healed instantly, delivered and set free because we find out what God is saying or doing in the current situation, then we say or do it. We incline our ear in the spiritual realm to find out how the Lord wants us to minister to them. We literally live, move and have our being in His glory, so the situation must change. Too many times we just start quoting Scriptures on healing or deliverance and nothing happens for that person. Why? Because Spirit and life must be breathed through your words and this can only happen if you say what Jesus is saying. This can only happen when you declare and perform the throne room conversation you hear. A Glory Walker revealed knows the days of laying hands on and praying for people with no results are over. The secret to guaranteed results have never been hidden from us. They have always been on display, but few ever venture into the realm of hearing throne room conversations and doing whatever He tells them to do. This is why so many needy people walk away from the prayer line the same way after prayer warriors spend ten minutes yelling and screaming with lengthy prayers. You have to learn to hear from God and do what He says, and they shall be healed, delivered and set free!

Do you want to be used by Jesus to do His works and even greater? Then you must make your way to the throne room. Your conversations are waiting for you right now. I encourage you to ask the Lord to start revealing your divine appointments each day. Ask Him to tell and show you what He is doing that day and let Him know that you want in on it. He will answer you and you will be a Glory Walker Revealed.

Praying & Fasting

As with anything in the kingdom, there is a price to pay. Knowing that there are throne room conversations available is not enough. We need to know how to have greater clarity concerning these conversations. As mentioned, asking Him for them is one element but there is a spiritual level which can only be tapped into through fasting and prayer. We must learn how to train our ears and eyes in the realm of the spirit, so we can effectively minister to those God will cause us to encounter. A life of prayer and fasting is the only way to stay in the spirit. Fasting and prayer has a way of quieting every other voice, so His becomes louder and clearer. By prayer, I am talking specifically about praying in your heavenly language. I realize there are various types of prayer, but I am only referring to this type right now. You must be filled with the Spirit with the evidence of speaking in tongues to tap into this realm. Religion and tradition would have you to believe this dispensation has passed away, but I assure you the baptism of the Holy Spirit is for right now, for every believer. Even Paul said, "**I thank God I speak in tongues more than you all (1 Corinthians 14:18)."** As Christians, we think we have to have a class for everything. Jesus never taught a class on being filled with the Holy Spirit. He simply told the disciples to wait in the upper room and they would receive the gift, the Holy Spirit, the promise of the Father. This is another essential aspect of walking in power and accessing throne room conversations. Every Glory Walker must be filled with the Holy Spirit with the evidence of speaking in tongues in order to walk in this dimension of the kingdom

When I began to be used by the Lord to release His glory, He told me that I must live a fasted life. I was already used to praying over an hour a day (not all at one time) in my heavenly language. This valuable guidance came through my spiritual dad, Dr. Nasir Siddiki. He challenged his spiritual sons and daughters to commit to praying an hour a day, with a promise of greater clarity in the spiritual realm. It was this level of prayer coupled with fasting two to three days per week that catapulted my hunger for the Lord. It was also this level of prayer and fasting which fine-tuned my ability to hear those throne room conversations and gave me the boldness to act on them. Even today, after two years, I continue to live a fasted life and pray in my heavenly language daily. As a result, God is using me to impact people's lives in so many ways. In my world, this is really all that matters to me. There is no substitute for seeing people encounter the Living God.

Today, you can decide to move to another level in the realm of the spirit. Make yourself available to get insider information from the throne room of Heaven by living a life of fasting and prayer. Your Father is waiting for you to manifest His glory in the earth.

Chapter Ten

Persecution Awaits You

There are a lot of people who claim they want others to succeed or excel in the things of God but when they see them start to rise to another level in the Spirit, pride, jealousy, envy, offense and religious tradition will rear its ugly head. I am not talking about this from the position of a spectator, but from first-hand experience. I endured a great deal of religious pressure and persecution because of the new place I had found with God. What made it even more difficult was the fact that it came from people whom I loved. Not only was I persecuted but so were others who longed for more. They were also dealt with in a very ungodly manner. Persecution came from pastors and leaders because they were too busy vying for attention. It came from people I had poured out my life for - for years. I made sure I never delivered a word that did not come from the mouth of God. I had labored over every detail of ministering the Word to the people on Wednesday and Sunday mornings. I was under the impression this was what believers and pastors, of all people, wanted. I thought we all wanted a fresh encounter with the

Jesus we read about in our Bible. I had no clue that panting after God would put me in a place like this. I intentionally have left this segment towards the end of the book. I want you to be aware, that should you decide to become a Glory Walker Revealed, persecution awaits you on every turn. Should you decide to pant after and passionately pursue His presence, persecution, in this life will come. Abandoning all for His glory is the requirement for a Glory Walker. You must be willing to allow the Lord to dismantle your associations and influences if you really want to experience His glory. Can you imagine my sheer disappointment when I found out that all most believers/pastors really want is an institution called church, instead of a genuine move of the Holy Spirit, marked by a demonstration of His power!

In the midst of my persecution, God began to send me spiritual sons and daughters. I promise you I never asked for them, God just sent them! It was a very uncomfortable, weighty and humbling experience. I have a very direct no-nonsense personality, so what you see is what you get. Some people, before they got to know me, said I seemed unapproachable. Though that is very far from the truth, what I really am is guarded about who I let in my circle of influence. But my sons and daughters could see past my tough exterior and connect spiritually. God sent them to love me, receive an impartation of His anointing, to share fresh revelation with them and to reconnect them with the Living God in a way they had not yet experienced. From the outside I looked the same, except for the twenty pounds I lost while I was fasting; but on the inside I was another person. My spirit had been renewed and the glory of God that had been released on the inside of me was like a magnet which was attracting them. They were also panting after God and willing to and did undergo the persecution which accompanied their thirst.

There is one characteristic about religious tradition which can't be denied, it always leaves you thirsty. Religion & tradition **ALWAYS** leaves you empty and wanting, like the Samaritan woman at the well who needed living water. Believers across the nation have settled for the programs and mechanics of church, and are spiritually dehydrated and don't even know it. Their spirits are crying out for the Living Water, but their spiritual busyness has them so preoccupied, that they can't address the cry of their own heart! Now please let me say, I am not against the local church; it is necessary for the growth, equipping and release of disciples to carry out the call of Christ. To be at odds with the church would put me at odds with the Lord Jesus Christ and the will of the Father. I am however, against the agenda to push big buildings, cafes, bookstores and programs as a means to pacify and preoccupy people when it is evident that the anointing and presence of the Holy Spirit is not in the house. Substituting God with stuff and calling it church is a very sore spot for me. Keep all of that stuff and give me the glory of God. I will take a meeting at a warehouse where the manifest presence of God shows up, over a beautifully decorated building anytime. Do you know why people will walk away from the form of godliness and pant after God? They do so because they have an overwhelming thirst for the presence of God more than anything else men can give them. Panters, are people who recognize their desperate need for God above everything else, even though they are aware of the persecution that awaits them. The persecution which awaits you pales in comparison to the glory which will be revealed in and through you.

Chapter Eleven

My Journey Continues

As I type this last, but not final chapter of my journey, I must tell you, I am loving my life and relationship with the Lord. I am currently Pastor of Oil & the Glory Ministries Wisdom Center of Clermont, along with my spiritual daughter and Co-Pastor Shirmeka Peden. I assure you things have not been easy, and we have suffered much at the hands of those who could not discern the time of the return of the glory of the Lord. Regardless, we would not change a thing. I believe every aspect was a necessary part of our assignment. It was necessary for us to suffer a little while to be made strong, steadfast and firm.

I want to take a moment to mention a lady by the name of Ms. Mae. I promised in one of the chapters to share one of the good conversations that were being said about me. Upon my exit from my former church, as I headed to start my ministry, this wonderful woman of God stopped me outside to talk for a moment. She had tears in her eyes and she said, "I knew it. I knew you could not stay. When you were on the platform being released I wanted to jump up and say, I knew it! Sometimes we never realize what we have until it leaves us." She apologized for being judgmental. I did not even know she felt that way!

Below is a message she sent me a few months later:

I am really going to miss your spirit, your wisdom and your love for God. You know sometimes we have it right before us and do not see it, and do not know how to appreciate it. Instead of absorbing we push it away. Actually, I am talking about myself, because I feel the guilt of being hard hearted at times. That was so wrong. I want to ask for forgiveness for all the wrong thoughts. I pray that God will always keep His arms around you and give you all your heart desires.

She blessed me so much that day. I told her I would talk about her in my next book and I have kept my word. God is so good!

A Demonstration of Power- Glory Walkers Revealed

As a result of the impartation of this glory anointing, many healings have occurred through our hands. I have also, along with my daughter Shirmeka, stayed true to the promise made to the Lord not to hoard the oil. As He directs, we release this anointing as we travel or during our Hosting His presence encounters. This is a platform where we set the atmosphere for people to encounter the abiding presence of God. During Hosting His Presence we have an encounter through worship, an impartation of anointing and a demonstration of His power, characterized by words of knowledge, healing, and deliverance.

I will take the rest of this chapter to share with you a few of the great works the Lord has performed through us.

Deliverance from Drugs & Back Healed

There was a young man who was addicted to prescription drugs. He found himself in an out of prison because he was stealing to support his habit. One Sunday morning during worship, the Holy Spirit told me He was going to deliver Him that day. I walked over to him and shared what the Lord said to me. Upon hearing this, He wanted to be delivered. I laid hands on him, and have never seen anyone fall like that before. He went down in slow motion, as if he was literally in someone's arms. At the end of the service he told me he felt like he was in God's arms. He also wanted healing for his back, which was the cause of the continuous pain and subsequent dependence on prescription drugs. The doctors told him surgery was his only alternative. I laid hands on him and commanded his back to be healed. I asked him how he felt. He said his back felt tight. At that moment the Lord dropped a word of knowledge in my spirit and said, "I am tightening his spine right now." I had him bend down and move and he was healed. His spine was still tight because the anointing was at work. The next day I saw Him and his back was no longer tight.

A week later, I was home in my bathroom getting ready to go out. The Lord called this young man's name out to me and said he was going to grow his leg out. When I saw Him that Sunday after service, I shared with him what the Lord has said. He had a slight limp, but I never gave it any thought. I had him sit in a seat and began to command the leg to grow out. The Lord dropped a word of knowledge in my spirit about a groin injury he sustained during his youth. When I released that word from my mouth, his leg grew out instantly! He got up and started walking fast, then he started running! He also showed me some karate moves that he had been unable to do for years. God is amazing and I give Him all of the glory.

Enlarged Heart Healed

There was a woman, perhaps in her 60's, who had an enlarged heart. She came forward with her daughter, who was crying because of her mom's condition. Ms. Pat, Pastor Shirmeka and I laid hands on her and commanded her heart to be normal in Jesus' name. She went to the doctor the next day and her heart was perfectly normal! May all of the glory be given to our amazing God!

Eyes Healed During Worship

One Thursday during one of our Bible studies we entered a very unique realm where the presence and Glory of God was so strong. After worship we began our Bible study. The instruction was given to turn to the Bible reference for the evening. After service one of the ladies came up and said she went to put her glasses on to find the Bible reference and realized her eyes had been healed and restored in the atmosphere of the glory, during worship. She no longer needed her glasses to read! We can only give God the glory!

Gospel Event Turned Healing Service

Pastor Shirmeka was ministering at a gospel event/ dinner and I accompanied her. After she ministered there was a segment when the Lord was speaking to both of us at the same time. He said healing was going to break out. I had no idea the Lord was speaking to her, nor did she know the same thing was going on with me! What were we to do? The Holy Spirit is a gentleman, so we both had resolved that if God wanted to manifest healing He was going to orchestrate the entrance of it. Again, neither of us knew that God was saying the same thing to both of us at the same time. I saw her get up from her seat and head to the back to talk to the pastor's wife. They started moving towards the front and Pastor Shirmeka came back to her seat. I did not know it, but She had shared what the Lord said with the pastor's wife, but nothing was done. The next thing I knew the pastor started closing out, but God put a prophetic word in his mouth. He called both of us up and began to prophesy over us. What an arrangement by God! When he was done, I went up to him and said the Lord wants to manifest healing. He handed me the mic. All I can say is, my daughter and I were used by God to see so many people instantly healed that night. Backs were healed, bodies made whole, eyes healed, demonic spirits were cast out, and a stroke victim was made whole! They thought they were having a gospel/dinner concert, but God had other plans. Again, we give God the glory due His name.

Healing from Rectal Cancer

The brother of a young lady I knew was diagnosed with rectal cancer. She had moved out of the area, but I saw her posts on Facebook concerning her brother. I sent her a message and asked her to bring her brother to our Bible study. They had one obstacle after another and just could not seem to get there. One night after Bible study I was on Facebook and the Lord told me to message her and tell her I would travel to meet with her brother and pray for his healing. We set a day and time. On my way, I asked the Lord to allow this man to feel His touch and know when the cancer leaves His body. I met with him. We talked for quite a while and then I laid hands on him and commanded the cancer to leave his body. I assured him I felt the anointing flow through my hands and he was healed. We talked for a few minutes and he said, "I don't know if I should say it, but I felt something leave my body, there where the cancer was." We stopped and praised God. A few days later my daughter and I traveled to Louisiana for a ministry trip and I received a message that the gentleman's rectal bleeding had stopped. About a month later she sent a message to confirm that her brother's tests showed he was totally cancer free. Even without the test results we already knew he was whole. May our Lord be glorified!

Hosting His Presence

At our most recent Hosting His Presence encounter, the Lord began to use Pastor Shirmeka and myself to minister healing. Everyone was healed that night. There was a lady in particular whose whole body was in pain because of some sort of an accident she had suffered. Her whole body was affected. She also wore a back brace. We laid hands on her and began to speak to her body, spine etc., in the name of Jesus, and she was instantly healed. She went and took off her brace and gave God the glory!

Financial Breakthrough

One Sunday as I closed out service, the Holy Spirit gave me a word of knowledge for tithers whose finances were being blocked. I called them up and began to lay hands on them and release their finances. There was a young lady whose husband had a business, and it was very sluggish. I laid hands on her and spoke the words God put in my mouth. I saw her a few days later and she testified that the next day, the flood gates of heaven opened in that business. Her husband had so much business he could not handle it all. Our faithful God never disappoints!

Closing Remarks

My friend, the realm of the glory is an amazing place to be in. It's a realm where everything is expedited. In the glory manifestations are instant and effortless. We have seen the hand of God move in such a mighty way over the last two years. There isn't a greater joy in this earth than to see people's lives radically changed by a genuine encounter with the Living God. Even after all I have experienced, I am still panting after Him. I have only begun my journey. The Lord has promised me forty years of ministry; characterized by the oil of His anointing, the presence of His glory, and a demonstration of His power. Now it's your turn. God is calling you to arise out of the ashes of religion and tradition. He is drawing you, by His Spirit, to become a vessel He can flow through. I speak to the dead bones of your life and declare you will yet live again. You are part of the remnant who will walk this earth and release the knowledge of the glory of the Lord as the waters cover the sea.

As you come to the close of this God breathed account, I command the Glory Walker in you to arise. May the consuming fire of the Living God be ignited from deep within you and may it be as a fire shut up in your bones. May a hunger and thirst for Him be birthed in you from this day forward. May you passionately pursue an intentional encounter with Him daily and never return again to church as usual. May the Glory Walker in you be revealed!

God Bless you,
Pastor Sonya L. Thompson

ABOUT THE AUTHOR

Minister Sonya L. Thompson has been teaching the word in some capacity for almost 16 years. In the summer of 2013 She became consumed with the desire to encounter the God of the Bible in a whole new way. Sonya became tired of the "mechanics" of  church and its programs and longed for an intentional, dynamic, daily encounter with the Holy Spirit. During an extended time of fasting and prayer, the Holy Spirit spoke two words into her spirit, "Azusa Street." That was the turning point of her life. After researching and reading on this glorious era in our history, she cried out to God for this kind of anointing for her life and those around her. God answered that call in December of 2013 by sending her to meet with Brother Tommy Welchel, one of the last survivors who carried the Azusa Street anointing. He received an impartation of those anointings from the participants of Azusa Street. In mid December of 2013, Sonya, along with her colleague and ministry partner, Mrs. Pat Hart went to Arizona to receive the Azusa Street anointing. As a result, Minister Sonya's ministry is characterized by the presence/glory of God, His anointing, and a powerful demonstration of the Holy Spirit whenever she teaches. No one's life remains the same after connecting with and sitting under this anointing! She is currently the Pastor of Oil & The Glory Ministries Wisdom Center of Clermont, in Clermont, Florida.

She is called to "Train, Educate and Advise through the Gospel with Simplicity and Purity." She is ordained by world renowned minister of the gospel, Dr. Nasir Siddiki. Sonya is a biblical teacher, entrepreneur, mentor and business owner. She holds a B.S. degree in the field of Business Administration. Sonya is the founder of Vanguard Theological Seminary and lead consultant at OTG Consulting, which is a full service ministry consultation firm. She is also a bestselling self published author of "Business By The Bible," "Seeds of Prosperity," "Break Out of Poverty Into Financial Abundance" and Declare Yourself Wealthy." She has been a key note speaker at several ministry conferences and a special guest on many Christian radio and TV stations. She recently appeared as a special guest on "With God You Will Succeed", with speaker and teacher Dr. Tom Leding.

Sonya is driven to, Introduce people to the Living God; To lead others to encounter the abiding presence of God in a way which will forever change their lives; and to impart the anointing which has freely been graced upon her, into the lives of others as led by the Holy Spirit. She has been married to Chris for 25 years and has a son, Aaron.

BOOKS BY SONYA L. THOMPSON

Business By The Bible
Seeds of Prosperity Book & CD
Break Out of Poverty Into Financial Abundance
Declare Yourself Wealthy
Declare Yourself Wealthy Journal

www.oilandtheglory.com

Also Available on Amazon

For booking or to schedule a Hosting His presence encounter at your church, please contact our ministry office 352.223.6290 or email encounter@oilandtheglory.com

Made in the USA
Columbia, SC
25 August 2019